FOREVER living without YOU

Jo Hope

BookLeaf Publishing

India | USA | UK

Presentation by *BookLeaf Publishing*

Web: www.bookleafpub.com

E-mail: info@bookleafpub.com

ISBN: 9789363313750

First edition 2024

DEDICATION

For all of you that have loved, lost and continue every minute of every day to cope with that loss – grief is a place of sanctuary, where we are free to feel, for however long the journey takes us.

ACKNOWLEDGEMENT

There's a certain irony that my second collection of poetry focuses on loss – and the many guises that can present themselves to us as – when, whilst publishing, I've recently lived through the life-changing loss of my therapy dog.

No amount of studying, researching, obtaining certificates of achievement or reflecting on past losses can ever fully offset the short, sharp slap in the face that death brings; no amount.

Neither reading my own work back to me nor listening to my audio pieces; it has all been words and noise.

I know I won't always feel like I do right now – forever.

I've always believed in the ebbs and flows of life, love and loss and have always believed in my own ability to drag myself up and out of my pit of despair.

Except now I have to do it without my girl beside me.

My Lotto couldn't ever verbalise her support, but I hope I will always remember the learnings of her love.

She was my therapist for nearly 11 wholesome years. She saw me through the most impactful events of my life and had done more for me than any amount of medicine or psychotherapy could.

It's a difficult transition, but I would never do her the disservice of forgetting and giving up on all her hard work.

PREFACE

'Nothing comes easy, nothing…

I often reflect on the length of time it took to purposefully drag myself out of the darkness I was in.

We might fall into our dark despair quickly – but crawling back out takes strength; it takes determination; it takes clinging on with bloodied fingertips and dragging grazed knees and no matter what, we find the strength to keep on going.'

:Hope

One Last Time

I want to talk to you,
and hear about your day
I want to sit and listen,
to all the things you might not say.

I want to know your secrets,
your happiness,
your fears
I want to be there for you,
for the sadness
and the tears.

I want to remember,
how it feels to have a chat
We'd often talk about nothing,
lots of this and bits of that.

I want to know where you are now,
but I know I'll never know,
we were so young when your time had come,
and you simply
had
to
go.

I really want to talk to you,
and hear about your day
I'll never truly understand
why you had to leave and couldn't stay.

Letting Go

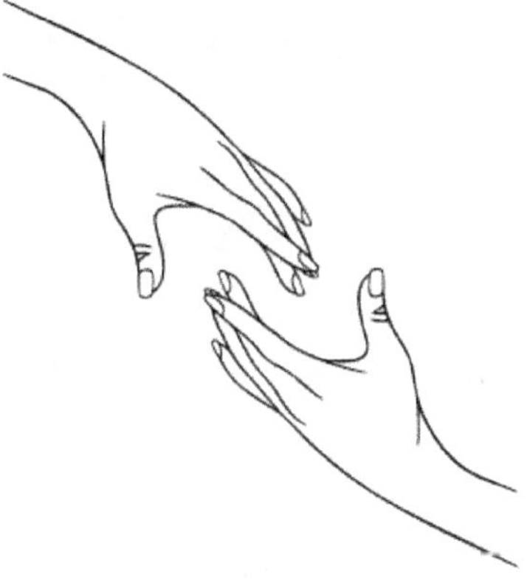

I wasn't ready

I wasn't ready for you to leave
I wasn't ready for you to leave my life

I wasn't ready for you to give up
I wasn't ready for you to give up on me
I wasn't ready for you to give up on us

I wasn't ready for you to no longer care
I wasn't ready for you to no longer be there

I wasn't ready for you to walk away
I wasn't ready for you to not stay

I wasn't ready for you to leave
I wasn't ready for you to leave me

alone,
lonely,
lost,
afraid

I wasn't ready.

Healing Time

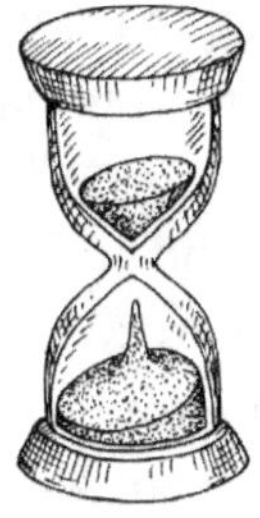

They say, 'Time is a healer'.
I'm not sure that is true
it doesn't feel like healing
when I'm missing you.

They say, 'It does get easier'.
and sometimes that is so
but it's still so hard to comprehend
how I had to let you go.

The minutes turn into hours
and the hours turn into days
I find myself reminiscing
but then something distracts my gaze.

The rest of the world keeps turning
No one knows the pain inside
if 'it [really] does get easier'
then why do I need to hide…?

I want to talk about you
look at your photos in their frame
I never want there to be a day
when I don't speak of your name

They say, 'Time is a healer'.
I want to believe it's true
for time is what is missing
time that should be spent with you.

Signs of You

I see the stars in heaven
and count them two by two
there's one that shines so brightly
I wonder if it's you.

I notice a feather floating
it stops right at my feet
then skips along and dances
as I walk across the street.

A butterfly lands near me
it spreads its wings so bright
all your favourite colours there
before leaving to take flight.

I feel the gentle patter of rain
whilst the sun still shines
a rainbow arcs across the sky
surely it's a sign?

I see the stars in heaven
and count them two by two
there's one that shines so brightly
the one that shines for you.

Beside Me

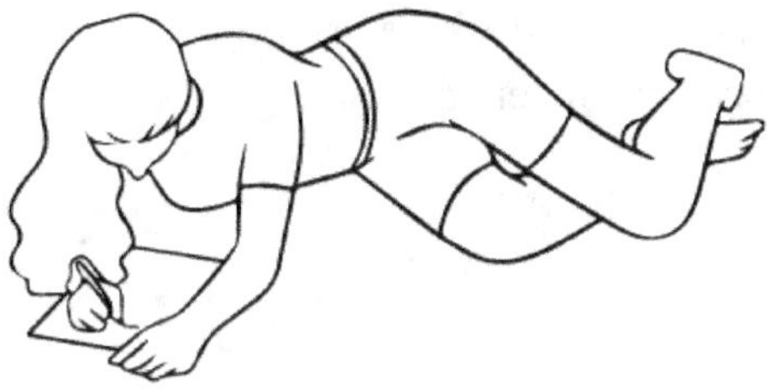

I think about you always
and today will be the same
just as the sun will shine brightly
after the relentless rain.

We'd watch sunrises after dark nights
and look for sunsets on endless tough days
and of course the perpetual cycle of life
still goes on and will not ever change.

Life was meaningful with you beside me
always effortless when you were near
you were my strength, my hopes,
my future dreams, everything I held so dear.

So I carry on my journey without you
and just talk to you in my head
there's so much more I could tell you
but I'll scribble it down instead.

I think about you always
and today will be the same
just as the sun will shine brightly
whenever we meet again.

Without and Within

Forever without
Forever within
How do I ever begin?

To face the day without you
To comfort the pain within me

A future of unspent memories
Has gone

Forever without
Forever within
How do I ever begin?

To be strong enough without you
To accept the pain within me

A future of changed memories
Has come

Forever without
Forever within
How do I ever begin?

To learn to live without you
To heal the pain within me

A future of contrasting memories
Has overcome

Forever without
Forever within
How do I ever begin?

To face the day
To comfort the pain

To be strong enough
To accept the pain

To learn to live
To heal the pain

A future of new memories
Has begun

Birthday Memories

It's your birthday up in heaven,
I wonder what it's like.

We've no gifts to wrap or cards to write
and the only candles that we'll light
will be the ones next to your photo,
in a frame on the side.

It's your birthday up in heaven,
I wonder what it's like.

No birthday wishes or happy returns
and instead, we'll quietly remember
the years before you said goodbye and
went to sleep forever.

It's your birthday up in heaven,
I wonder what it's like.

I hope there'll be music and dancing,
singing the whole day through,
much happiness and laughter;
they were the birthdays we had with you.

We remember all of the happy days
marking every year of your life.

You'll forever be the age when you left us–
and in our minds, we know time stood still
but in our hearts, we like to say 'Happy
Birthday',
and on this day we always will.

My Cat

I lost my cat
I didn't even know how to feel about that
losing my cat…

My cat
He was my cat

My brother in fur
My brother in my heart

And now my heart
Was broken in two
I'd had you since I was two

And
Then
You
Died

and I cried and cried
and died inside

I didn't even know
the how
or the why
or what I'd done
to have you leave my side

But the day you died
I died inside

I didn't know what to do
It broke my heart in two

To lose my best friend
who I'd known
since I was two

I loved you

and then just
like that

So abruptly

you were gone…

Like a Song

There has never been anyone like you;
and no one since you.
You were one of a kind,
a certain kind,
a mankind
and you were kind;
to me.

You were the 'big smile lights up a room' sort
who always had the funniest retort
to anything
and everything
I'd say.

You could dance
you could sing,
so much joy you would bring to my world
and then you asked me if I could be your best
girl…

You loved music, and it didn't matter where we
were,
you'd break out into song,
making me blush, but I didn't care
and still, I'd tag along.

I was too damaged
to take your hand in marriage,
you called me 'Joanne, you didn't want
everything (not a horse and not a carriage); you
simply wanted a "me"'.

Watching you,
is what I miss the most;
simply watching you
laughing,
smiling.
Hearing you,
seeing you…

We'd play the piano until we'd fall asleep
you told me your deepest secrets for me to keep.
You weren't afraid of anything,
not living,
and especially not of dying…

I torture myself about your last day on earth,
I often wonder how you felt
I hope you're up there looking down on me,
I still feel the urge to yell…

Why were you taken, Neill?
Why were you taken so young?
It hurts my heart to acknowledge and feel
that your life should have been saved and
replayed
like a song.

*Dedicated to my dear, dear Neill, who was
cruelly snatched from us; your memory will
always remain.

Lost Friends

Meet me at the table
a table set for two
We'll add a bench, a couple more chairs
we've room now for a few.

We'll chat about memories made
sing songs we used to know
Share photographs,
read old letters aloud,
of the 'good old days' so long ago.

Meet me at the table
a table set for two
I always whiled away the hours best,
when whiling away with you.

Meet me at the table
a table set for two
Most of you have now passed on,
which now leads me back to…

…chatting about the memories made
singing songs we used to know.
Sharing photographs, reading letters aloud;
telling you we loved you so.

So meet me at the table
a table set for two
I sit opposite your empty chair,
and feel the miss of you.

Grieving Waves

For all of you that have loved, lost
and continue every minute of every day
to cope with that loss,
please remember that it's okay to feel what
you're feeling right now.

It's okay to enjoy a happy day–when your grief
is nestling in the back of your mind.

It's most certainly okay to let the tears flow
when the moment hits you and you feel that
emptiness in your heart.

There's no time limit on grief, no fast-track
passes to purchase to rush you through.

Grief takes time,
healing takes time,
and if there is anything else I could add to this,
it's this: grief is absolutely personal and
individual.

Grieve in your own way,
never mind those who advise you that your
sadness should have expired.
Anyone who says such has most probably not
healed themselves.

Grief is a place of sanctuary, where we are free
to feel, for however long the journey takes us.

Grief is the only place we have to go when we
lose someone we love.

Guide You to the Light

I'd walk a mile in your shoes
even if the soles were worn
I'd listen intently to your voice
whilst you share your thoughts.

Your shoulders that are burdened with the
heaviness of life
I'd steady with my arms and hands and guide
you to the light.

It matters not how much the weight is you have
to carry
We'll share your worries, divide the load, a
problem halved so necessary.

Your shoulders that are burdened deserve to feel
so light
Without the pain and the darkness and heaviness
of life.

I'd walk a mile in your shoes
while you navigate your thoughts
Even with a heart and two soles that are tired
and tattered and worn.

It matters not how much the weight is you have
to carry
We'll share your worries, divide the load
between us,
I'll forever be your sanctuary.

Peace Release

There's an unspent anger occupying my mind
stuff I know I should leave behind

but

when the memories begin to swell
the pain I just cannot quell

I can't tell…
I can't tell…

no matter the freedom it would bring
no matter how my mind would be free to sing
free to sing about the things
that should bring
stillness

a welcome emptiness

a sense of cleansing

a sense of ending

a sense of the never-ending

unending peace

a release

piece by piece

of the need to feel at ease.

Simply Human

There are no rights,
no wrongs,
no decisions that can't be changed.

How you feel today is not how you'll feel
tomorrow or how you felt yesterday.

Healing – like most processes in life – is a
bittersweet mix of highs and lows,
it ebbs and flows;
some days we ride the waves, and others we
could easily drown.

It really is okay to not be over it,
to feel like you don't have it all together,
to experience the sorrow and the craziness over
and over again, but you will get there.

Let go of the control and trust the process.

Healing is messy,
but you're not;
you're simply human.

You've made it this far,
keep on going...

Forever Living Without You

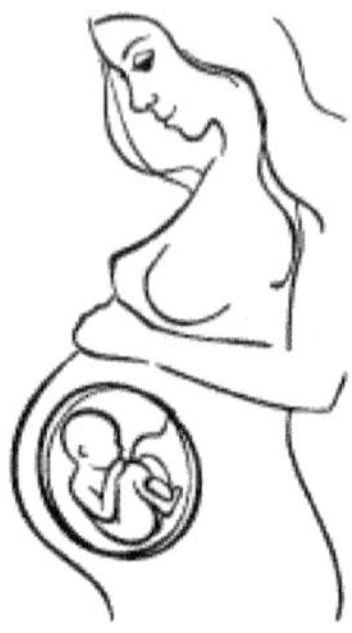

You were a part of me before I knew you –
before I knew what you had already begun to go
through.
Before your tiny being had the chance of life,
you changed the way I saw everything, and I
started to question 'why'?…

I didn't acknowledge your presence…
Maybe that was why..?

I didn't warmly welcome you…
Maybe that was why..?

I didn't know I was expectant…
Maybe that was why..?

I ate something I shouldn't…
Maybe that was why..?

I drank something I shouldn't…
Maybe that was why..?

I told myself I wasn't ready…
Maybe that was why..?

Maybe that was why you couldn't stay
Maybe that was why I heard them say:

'It wasn't
meant
to be
this way…'

When I heard them say you couldn't stay

It just wasn't
meant
to be
this way

Maybe that was why..?

You were a part of me before I even knew you–
I didn't know at that point what you had already
begun to go through.
Before your tiny being had the chance of life
You changed the way I saw everything, and I
started to question 'why'?…

They acknowledged your presence
They warmly welcomed you
They knew I was expectant
They knew it wasn't me, but you.

I hadn't eaten something I shouldn't
I hadn't drank something I shouldn't
But they told me you were not ready

That was why you couldn't stay,
That was why I heard them say

'It just wasn't
meant to be,
that your tiny being didn't grow enough
to eventually meet me'.

The Me You Wanted Me to Be

I walked away,
not in a blaze of awakening glory
but slowly,
thoughtfully…

I walked away,
gathered my things,
myself,
and my dignity
and I simply walked away…

I walked away when I began to see
that you wanted me not to be me – but a
different me – the 'me' you wanted me to be.

I walked away when I knew there was nothing
but control,
and an insidious resentment growing in my soul
and without fanfare and dramatics (no huge
drum roll…)
I walked away.

See, when someone chooses to tear you apart –
emotionally –
limb by limb,
breaking bones with their words,
leaving bruises with their silences,
splitting hairs,
their suspicions of you running wild in their
mind;
only to realise they have long been behind the
deep cuts to your very being…
Your existence day by day, chipped away;
moulding you into the idea of 'woman' that they
held onto so dear, for so long…

When someone casts you to one side
for their own worthless pride,
they're watching you die inside,
they know you have no choice but to hide, and
they simply
do
not
care.

They're too blinded to see,
by their own obscurity and
age-old insecurity;
they take your essence of purity
and make it their own…
and they'll continue to own and disown
until you are locked away inside your own head
and
alone…

So I walked away,
I had nowhere to go… it didn't matter that you
'loved me so';
having nowhere to go
was exactly
what
I needed
and
so

I walked away…

My Dad

My Dad liked purple shirts
and pink ties (and pretended to love the cat),
he loved singing,
musicals,
dancing – whilst 'acting the fool'
and making you laugh;
he was actually pretty good at all that.

My Dad had a smile,
a charm and a flair – that lit up the room you
walked in,
he'd mute the TV and share digestive biscuits –
which he kept by his chair in a tin.

My Dad had a presence,
always peaceful and calm,
it balanced out the day's chatter…
He loved a good chin-wag,
but the tales of your day – like his charm –
would be all that would matter.

My Dad had a depth of intelligence –
excited by quizzing
(whilst patiently puzzling),
competing together, always 'letting me win' – so
he said…
always knew he was kidding.

My Dad was my Dad, and I'm glad…

Wherever he is – on this 'his' day – I shall
quietly remember him as he'd eloquently say
'did you know I was born on the same day as the
Queen…'?
and take you with him on the seventy-plus years
of life that had been.

I can still imagine him sharing a brew,
with our dear Queen
and whispering to her, so all would hear:
'I had the same birthday as you'!

My Dad…

Exhale the Loss

I've often felt invisible,
but none more-so than when
my life – as I knew it – began to fall apart;
and there was no choice but to start again.

See, when you have been stripped
of everything you've always been
you want to hide yourself away
you absolutely don't want to be seen…

Loss isn't just about losing 'them'
it's also about losing 'self'.
Your identity
Your career
Your way of life
I was told it was 'best for my health'.

When you surrender your independence
and it's fundamentally against your will
there's no future in the distance ahead
time stops,
falls silent;
stands still.

The days merge into nights
and the dark hours dawn into new days,
everything ultimately becomes a blur
and I can't begin to count the ways;

that I would often wish…

how I would often wish…

Oh, so many times I would wish
I could sleep and never wake
because I hadn't the strength to face
yet another day.

Another day,
of living
in this peculiar way
of nothingness…

But the stark truth of the matter,
is that as much as it felt like forever,
I was able to pick up and gather,

gather myself,
my thoughts
and my resolve.

I was able to navigate the new path
in a way, I'd not had to before
I dragged myself up and out of my hole
and began to tiptoe in search of a new door.

I knocked on it with all my might
at some ridiculous hour of the night
…and of course, my knock wasn't answered.

So, I waited,
I waited for the morning light
and with rested eyes,
I searched until I began to discover
a whole row that looked just right…

and there it was,
a bright new door;
decorated in the brightest colours
– brighter than I'd ever seen before.

The door was big,
and bold
and striking;
I wasn't sure it was to my liking
but it was ajar…

I pushed at it with all the strength I had
to peer around it,
oh my, what a beautiful sight to be had
– I could see a future – my future – albeit far…

In that moment, I exhaled,
and lowered myself to the ground.
In spite of everything I'd lived through,
a new life was there;
just waiting to be found…

May You Always Remember

May you always remember you're not ever completely alone – please know that whilst I cannot always say I understand, believe me when I say, 'I hear you'.

May you always remember your emotions right now are completely valid, and if they're doing their best to bring you down, believe me when I say, 'I see you'.

May you recognise them,
May you notice them,
May you sit with them,
May you allow your mind to process,
May you allow yourself some space to just be,
May you feel this
moment,
and
May you breathe…

May you remember how you don't have to have
everything all figured out at once because
everything takes time.

May you remember gentle healing and consider
recovery from such losses takes time.

May you feel able to be kind to yourself, give
yourself some warm brushes of comfort; you
have made it to another day.

May you move now, feeling the best you can be,
and may you allow me to send strength to carry
you forward as you progress through your day.
May you always remember…

Would You..?

Would you dance me to the end of forever,
if I asked you to?
Would you sit with me in the moonlight,
and talk the whole night through?

Would you tell me your treasured stories?
Sing me your favourite songs?
Share your innermost secrets that you wouldn't
tell anyone?

Would you dance me to the end of forever,
if I asked you to?
Would you sit with me and count the stars and
share a brew or two?

Why make small talk about the weather when
time is all ours and can be erased.
There's a raw beauty in the details we can share
in these small ways.

Would you dance me to the end of forever,
if I asked you to?
I'd like to hear your stories and discover what
makes you, you.

Gone Forever

Door slam
Traffic jam

Stopped clock
Don't stop

Abruptness

Sadness

Madness

A full stop
This needs to stop

You were gone
I couldn't run

Couldn't chase you,
couldn't reach you,
I was so close
So close

You were gone
You were gone

Gone
Gone forever

Now it's only never

Never

Ever

No more calls
Just more walls

Between the here
and the now

and the then
and the when
and when will I ever see you again?

It hits me again
And again

And again

When will it end?

Will it end?

Before the end?

Before I end?

The End